STUDY GUIDE

YES!!!

For foreign and subsidiary rights, contact the author.

Cover design by: Sara Young
Cover photo by: Keith Betters

ISBN: 978-1-964794-51-8   1 2 3 4 5 6 7 8 9 10

Printed in the United States of America

STUDY GUIDE

YES!!!

CHRIS BINION

AVAIL

CONTENTS

CHAPTER ONE

YOUR ENCOUNTER

1

God wants to bless us far more than we want His blessing.

REVIEW, REFLECT, AND RESPOND

As you read Chapter 1: "Your Encounter" in
YES!!!, review, reflect on, and respond to the text
by answering the following questions.

As believers, we can sometimes be present in church but emotionally disconnected from God. Have you ever experienced that kind of disconnection? What do you think caused it?

_____

_____

_____

_____

_____

_____

_____

_____

What kind of neglect do you need to name and address in your relationship with God?

_____

_____

_____

_____

_____

_____

_____

_____

> *"Eye has not seen, nor ear heard, nor have entered into the heart of man the things which God has prepared for those who love Him."*
>
> **—1 Corinthians 2:9 (NKJV)**

Consider the scripture above and answer the following questions:

If God's plans for your life are greater than you can imagine, what makes it difficult for you to trust Him without seeing the full picture?

_____

_____

_____

_____

_____

_____

This verse speaks to the extravagant goodness of God. What do your decisions and mindset currently say about how much you believe He wants good things for you?

_____

_____

_____

_____

_____

_____

Think back to a time you sensed God asking you to do something, and you hesitated. What did that moment reveal about your trust in Him? What happened as a result?

_____

_____

_____

_____

_____

_____

This chapter is filled with examples of obedience before clarity. Where in your life are you demanding clarity before you're willing to say "yes"?

_____

_____

_____

_____

_____

_____

Where in your life do you need to move from passive hope to active pursuit?

_____

_____

_____

_____

_____

What's one moment where you knew you were being tested—whether in faith, leadership, or marriage—and your response became a turning point? What did it teach you about yourself?

_____

_____

_____

_____

_____

What's one area where you've been tempted to chase worldly affirmation rather than Kingdom obedience? Why?

_____

_____

_____

_____

_____

When have you treated God like a backup plan or fire insurance—something to run to when life gets hard rather than someone to walk with daily? What does it look like to flip that pattern?

_____

_____

_____

_____

_____

What hesitation, excuse, or delay has become instinctual for you—and how can you disrupt that cycle?

_____

_____

_____

_____

_____

If saying "yes" is less about spiritual adrenaline and more about faithful repetition, what's one small "yes" you can say to God this week?

_____

_____

_____

_____

_____

CHAPTER TWO

YOUR "YES!!!" CHANGES EVERYTHING

We don't hold God in our hands; He holds us in His.

REVIEW, REFLECT, AND RESPOND

As you read Chapter 2: "Your 'YES!!!' Changes Everything" in *YES!!!*, review, reflect on, and respond to the text by answering the following questions

What jail-cell moment—literal or metaphorical—has most shaped your story? Where do you find yourself saying "yes" to God, and where did you find yourself saying "no"?

_____

_____

_____

_____

_____

_____

_____

_____

When has God broken into your life during a moment that seemed impossible, unredeemable, or out of control?

_____

_____

_____

_____

_____

_____

_____

_____

> *"For all the promises of God in Him are Yes, and in Him Amen, to the glory of God through us."*
>
> **—2 Corinthians 1:20 (NKJV)**

Consider the scripture above and answer the following questions:

This verse reminds us that God never makes a promise He doesn't intend to keep. What promise from God have you struggled to believe still applies to you?

_____

_____

_____

_____

_____

_____

_____

If every promise in Christ is already "Yes," what limiting belief, fear, or unresolved pain is still causing you to live like it's a "maybe"?

_____

_____

_____

_____

_____

_____

_____

In what ways have you forgotten that God's invitation began long before your obedience?

_____

_____

_____

_____

_____

_____

Where in your leadership or life have you resisted God's direction because it didn't align with logic or appearances?

_____

_____

_____

_____

_____

_____

Who in your life or team is ready for a second chance—and are you willing to give it?

_____

_____

_____

_____

_____

_____

Where do you need to believe God can rewrite someone's—or your own—story?

_____

_____

_____

_____

_____

_____

What's one area where you've been trying to maintain control rather than resting in that truth?

_____

_____

_____

_____

When you look at how you spend your time, money, and emotional energy, what priorities do they reveal? Are those aligned with your "Yes!" to Jesus—or calling it into question?

_____

_____

_____

_____

_____

What old "clothes" (habits, relationships, patterns) have you struggled to take off—despite knowing God has something new for you to put on?

_____

_____

_____

_____

_____

The chapter ends by describing how transformation changes everything: our connection with God, our priorities, relationships, habits, and generosity. Which of these areas is currently the most resistant to change in your life—and why?

_____

_____

_____

_____

_____

THE JOURNEY OF SURPRISES

3

Sometimes, God surprises us with instructions that seem to make no sense—especially if someone else offers a more reasonable path.

REVIEW, REFLECT, AND RESPOND

As you read Chapter 3: "The Journey of Surprises" in *YES!!!*, review, reflect on, and respond to the text by answering the following questions.

What's a moment in your life where you expected one outcome, but God delivered something radically better? What did it reveal about how you view His power and promises?

_____

_____

_____

_____

_____

_____

_____

_____

Where in your leadership or relationships have you given up too soon—convinced that God wouldn't or couldn't move? What might He still want to surprise you with?

_____

_____

_____

_____

_____

_____

_____

_____

> *"Now to Him who is able to do exceedingly abundantly above all that we ask or think, according to the power that works in us."*
>
> **—Ephesians 3:20 (NKJV)**

Consider the scripture above and answer the following questions:

What's one area in your life where your prayers have been too small? How might God be inviting you to expand your expectations?

_____

_____

_____

_____

_____

_____

_____

This verse ties God's abundance to the power that works "in us." What area of your life are you tempted to pray for externally, while God may actually want to transform something internally?

_____

_____

_____

_____

_____

_____

_____

When has God asked you to do something that didn't make strategic or logical sense—but turned out to be divine? What did that obedience cost you? What did it teach you?

_____

_____

_____

_____

_____

_____

What's one situation in your past that you initially labeled as a disappointment—but later saw as a divine setup?

_____

_____

_____

_____

_____

_____

What "snake moment" in your life felt like spiritual warfare—
where everything seemed to backfire—until God revealed His
greater authority?

_____

_____

_____

_____

_____

Who in your life have you been praying for over the long haul
despite years of disappointment or estrangement? What
would it look like to keep showing up with faith for an "above
and beyond" kind of restoration?

_____

_____

_____

_____

_____

When have you hesitated to take a step forward because the
resources, people, or logistics didn't seem to be there? What
does this chapter say to that hesitation?

_____

_____

_____

_____

_____

What's a current limitation in your ministry or business that could actually be an invitation for God to provide in a surprising way?

_____

_____

_____

_____

_____

The chapter highlights how God doesn't just meet expectations—He exceeds them. What's one promise from Scripture that you've put on the shelf because it feels too extravagant?

_____

_____

_____

_____

God's surprises often involve using the least likely people in the most unlikely places. Who's someone you've discounted—maybe even yourself—who may be the very person God wants to use next?

_____

_____

_____

_____

_____

OBSTACLES ARE OPPORTUNITIES

4

Temptation is usually coupled with attractive lies.

REVIEW, REFLECT, AND RESPOND

As you read Chapter 4: "Obstacles Are Opportunities"
in *YES!!!*, review, reflect on, and respond to the
text by answering the following questions.

Where have you mistaken an obstacle as a sign that you're
on the wrong path—when, in reality, it may be your invitation
to persevere and trust God?

_____

_____

_____

_____

_____

_____

_____

What hardship in your life right now feels more like a threat
than an opportunity? What might shift if you asked God to
show you what He's developing in you through it?

_____

_____

_____

_____

_____

_____

_____

> *"You are My servant, I have chosen you and have not cast you away: Fear not, for I am with you; Be not dismayed, for I am your God. I will strengthen you, Yes, I will help you, I will uphold you with My righteous right hand."*
>
> **—Isaiah 41:9-10 (NKJV)**

Consider the scripture above and answer the following questions:

What burden are you carrying right now that would feel lighter if you really believed God was upholding you with His righteous right hand?

_____

_____

_____

_____

_____

_____

This passage reminds us that being chosen doesn't mean being spared from hardship. What evidence of God's help have you overlooked because you were focused on the pain?

_____

_____

_____

_____

_____

_____

What's one area of your life where obedience feels dangerous—and how is God asking you to keep going?

_____

_____

_____

_____

_____

The cycle of a dream includes birth, death, rebirth, and fulfillment. Where are you in that cycle right now—and what does faithfulness look like in this phase?

_____

_____

_____

_____

_____

The story of Daniel shows us that bold obedience will provoke resistance. What recent "lion's den" moment have you walked through—and what did it reveal about your faith?

_____

_____

_____

_____

_____

When has God allowed a dream to die in your life? What signs of new life are beginning to emerge—or need your attention to grow?

_____

_____

_____

_____

_____

What voice (internal or external) has been the loudest in your mind lately? Is it truth or a distraction from the enemy? How do you know?

_____

_____

_____

_____

_____

Where in your community or church is there pain that you're uniquely positioned to meet?

_____

_____

_____

_____

_____

Paul saw every hardship as a platform for ministry. What part of your current struggle could become someone else's breakthrough—if you're willing to share it?

_____

_____

_____

_____

_____

The enemy uses obstacles to drain us, but God uses them to refine us. What refinement is God working in your character through what you're facing right now?

_____

_____

_____

_____

_____

THE PROMISE IS A PROCESS

5

We hate to wait, but it's an integral part of how God refines our motives and prepares us for the next step.

REVIEW, REFLECT, AND RESPOND

As you read Chapter 5: "The Promise Is a Process"
in *YES!!!*, review, reflect on, and respond to the
text by answering the following questions.

What plan or exit strategy have you developed in your mind when God's timeline feels too long? What does that reveal about your expectations of Him?

_____

_____

_____

_____

_____

_____

_____

Where have you confused God's silence with His absence? How have you seen Him move even when you heard nothing? Provide an example.

_____

_____

_____

_____

_____

_____

_____

_____

Consider the scripture above and answer the following questions:

"My soul waits" implies more than outward obedience—it's a posture of the heart. Where has your soul been restless, anxious, or angry in the waiting?

_____

_____

_____

_____

_____

_____

The psalmist compares his waiting to a night watchman scanning the horizon for morning. What in your life feels like a long night, and what signs help you recognize when God is beginning to move—even if it's not the full breakthrough yet?

_____

_____

_____

_____

_____

_____

When have you assumed something was over—your ministry, a dream, a relationship—only to discover later that God was still in the process of fulfilling it?

_____

_____

_____

_____

_____

_____

What's one "yes" God asked you to give that had no immediate reward—but built the kind of endurance you couldn't have developed any other way?

_____

_____

_____

_____

_____

How has your internal dialogue changed during a season of waiting—either toward self-condemnation, resentment toward God, or growth in trust?

_____

_____

_____

_____

_____

What well-meaning advice or alternate path have others offered you during your waiting season? What did you choose, and was it the best choice? Why or why not?

_____

_____

_____

_____

_____

When have you tried to move to a different "table" before God told you it was time? What did that choice cost you—or what are you still unlearning from that moment?

_____

_____

_____

_____

_____

Waiting often exposes our motives. What deeper desire has God revealed in you during a season of silence or delay?

_____

_____

_____

_____

_____

Have you ever looked back on a waiting season and realized you were more focused on getting out of it than growing through it? What did you miss—or what did you finally see in hindsight?

_____

_____

_____

_____

_____

What story in this chapter most mirrored your own experience—and what did it convict or confirm about the process you're currently in?

_____

_____

_____

_____

_____

BELIEVING FOR THE UNBELIEVABLE

6

When we believe God will do a miracle, He sometimes takes us to a dead end before He opens the floodgates of heaven.

REVIEW, REFLECT, AND RESPOND

As you read Chapter 6: "Believing for the Unbelievable" in *YES!!!*, review, reflect on, and respond to the text by answering the following questions.

What's something you once believed was impossible—either in ministry, your family, or your personal healing—but now realize God was more than able to accomplish?

_____

_____

_____

_____

_____

_____

_____

What prayer or dream have you quietly stopped asking God for—not because He said "no," but because you stopped believing it was possible? What would it look like to start dreaming and praying again?

_____

_____

_____

_____

_____

_____

_____

> *"But Jesus looked at them and said to them, 'With men this is impossible, but with God all things are possible.'"*
> **—Matthew 19:26 (NKJV)**

Consider the scripture above and answer the following questions:

How has your definition of what's "possible" been shaped more by past disappointments than by God's promises?

_____

_____

_____

_____

_____

_____

_____

Jesus said these words in response to someone's question about who can be saved. What situation have you written off as irredeemable?

_____

_____

_____

_____

_____

_____

_____

_____

What "one day" dreams has God already put in your heart that you've delayed out of fear they're too big, too costly, or too impractical?

_____

_____

_____

_____

_____

_____

Think about a moment when you witnessed God do something miraculous for someone else. Did it stir faith, envy, or doubt in you—and what did you do with that reaction?

_____

_____

_____

_____

_____

_____

Think about the people in the chapter who received healing, restoration, deliverance, or transformation. Which story most closely mirrors something in your own life—and what part of that healing still feels incomplete?

_____

_____

_____

_____

_____

What do you fear more: believing God and being disappointed or not believing and missing out on what He wants to do?

_____

_____

_____

_____

_____

What would change if you led your team, your family, or your ministry from a place of expectation rather than caution?

_____

_____

_____

_____

_____

What emotional or spiritual resistance rises in you when you're asked to believe God for something big—skepticism, fear of disappointment, unworthiness? What's underneath that reaction?

_____

_____

_____

_____

_____

What does it reveal about your relationship with God when you find yourself more comfortable meeting others' needs than believing He wants to meet yours?

_____

_____

_____

_____

_____

If you were to write your own "unbelievable but true" testimony of what God has done, what story would you tell— and who needs to hear it?

_____

_____

_____

_____

_____

CHAPTER SEVEN

ON THE OTHER SIDE OF OBEDIENCE

The Lord didn't call me to understand.
He called me to trust Him.

REVIEW, REFLECT, AND RESPOND

As you read Chapter 7: "On the Other Side of Obedience" in *YES!!!*, review, reflect on, and respond to the text by answering the following questions.

Rahab's obedience changed her entire bloodline and played a role in the arrival of Jesus. Where in your life do you need to stop measuring obedience by what it will do for you and start asking what it could unlock for others?

_____

_____

_____

_____

_____

_____

_____

_____

Think about an act of obedience you've delayed not because of fear but because you didn't think it would matter. What's the potential hidden cost of continuing to underestimate its significance?

_____

_____

_____

_____

_____

_____

_____

_____

> *"You are My friends if you do whatever I command you. No longer do I call you servants, for a servant does not know what his master is doing; but I have called you friends, for all things that I heard from My Father I have made known to you."*
>
> **—John 15:14-15 (NKJV)**

Consider the scripture above and answer the following questions:

Jesus calls His friends into the loop of what the Father is doing. Where in your life do you feel spiritually "in the dark," and could that lack of insight be connected to a lack of surrendered obedience? How so?

_____

_____

_____

_____

_____

_____

This passage draws a line between knowing about Jesus and being entrusted by Him. Where do you see yourself on that spectrum—and what shift might He be inviting you into?

_____

_____

_____

_____

_____

_____

The story of Jericho shows God's power to demolish what man cannot. What "strategy" have you been clinging to that God may actually want to interrupt with His own unlikely plan?

_____

_____

_____

_____

_____

_____

Have you ever obeyed God in one area of your life while knowingly resisting Him in another? How has that split focus affected your peace, clarity, or growth?

_____

_____

_____

_____

_____

_____

The chapter emphasizes immediate obedience—especially when God repeats His instructions. What repeated nudge have you been brushing aside, and what might it cost to finally respond?

_____

_____

_____

_____

_____

Delayed obedience often disguises itself as "waiting for confirmation." When has that tendency in your life actually been a form of procrastination?

_____

_____

_____

_____

_____

Think about a past season where you disobeyed God. What were the relational or emotional ripple effects—not just for you but for the people around you?

_____

_____

_____

_____

_____

Jesus says He has made known "all things" from the Father. What parts of God's character or will became clearer to you only after you chose to obey something difficult?

_____

_____

_____

_____

_____

The Jewish tradition of Jubilee meant canceled debts and restored inheritance. What part of your story needs that kind of reset—and what act of obedience might begin that restoration?

_____

_____

_____

_____

_____

What is something God has asked you to create, share, or start—but you've hesitated because you think it's not your place or you're not ready?

_____

_____

_____

_____

_____

YOU HAVE MY "YES!!!"

8

> *God's anointing destroys the idolatrous yoke, and God's glory destroys the selfish agenda.*

REVIEW, REFLECT, AND RESPOND

As you read Chapter 8: "You Have My 'Yes!!!'" in
YES!!!, review, reflect on, and respond to the text
by answering the following questions.

When has your outward behavior suggested a "yes" to God
while your inner life continued saying "no"? How did that
internal conflict affect your peace or progress?

_____

_____

_____

_____

_____

_____

_____

_____

What consistent "yes" in your life has produced the greatest
spiritual momentum—and where has that momentum stalled?

_____

_____

_____

_____

_____

_____

_____

_____

> *"But be doers of the word, and not hearers only, deceiving yourselves."*
>
> **—James 1:22**

Consider the scripture above and answer the following questions:

According to this verse, hearing truth isn't the problem—doing it is. What truth from God's Word do you already know but haven't put into action?

_____

_____

_____

_____

_____

What personal area (your finances, marriage, habits, or leadership decisions) has been most affected by inaction disguised as obedience?

_____

_____

_____

_____

_____

Think of a time in the past when someone confirmed something God had already told you. How long did it take for you to act on it?

_____

_____

_____

_____

_____

How has your relationship with God changed as you've moved from being a consumer of His Word to a doer of it? What resistance do you still feel in making that shift permanent?

_____

_____

_____

_____

_____

What does your private thought life reveal about what you truly desire—and how does that align or conflict with what you say you want spiritually?

_____

_____

_____

_____

_____

When have you found yourself overcommitted to spiritual busyness while undercommitted to spiritual obedience? What changes does that conviction require?

_____

_____

_____

_____

_____

What specific "yes" would realign your life around God's agenda rather than your own comfort or achievement?

_____

_____

_____

_____

_____

In your life, where have you promoted values that you struggle to personally practice? What's one step you can take toward closing that gap?

_____

_____

_____

_____

_____

What personal idol—whether control, validation, comfort, or success—has God been calling you to surrender? How willing are you to do it? Explain.

_____

_____

_____

_____

_____

What kind of "spiritual double-mindedness" do you recognize in yourself—living torn between loyalty to God and loyalty to the approval of others?

_____

_____

_____

_____

_____

Which story, truth, or conviction from this book has stuck with you the most—and how will you allow it to reshape the way you live, lead, or listen to God?

_____

_____

_____

_____

_____

HAVE YOU GIVEN GOD YOUR YES!!!?

www.ingramcontent.com/pod-product-compliance
Lightning Source LLC
Chambersburg PA
CBHW070050100426
42734CB00040B/2976